My First Thai
People, Relationships & Adjectives

Picture Book with English Translations

Published By: AuthorUnlock.com

People & Relationships

เด็กทารก

Dek - Ta - Rok

Baby

พี่ชาย

Phee - Chai

Brother

ลูกสาว
Look - Saw
Daughter

พ่อ

Pho

Father

เพื่อน

Phoen

Friend

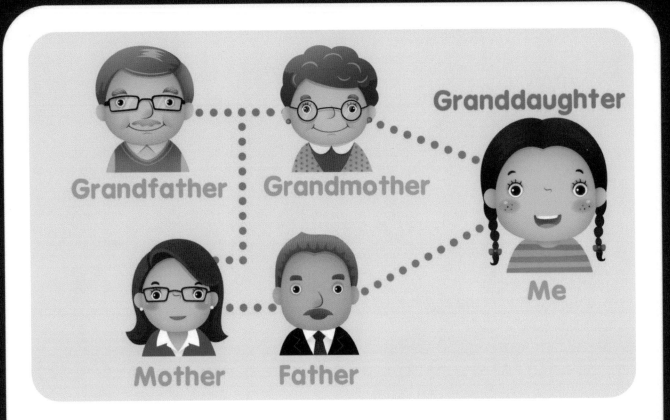

หลานสาว

Lhan – Saw

Granddaughter

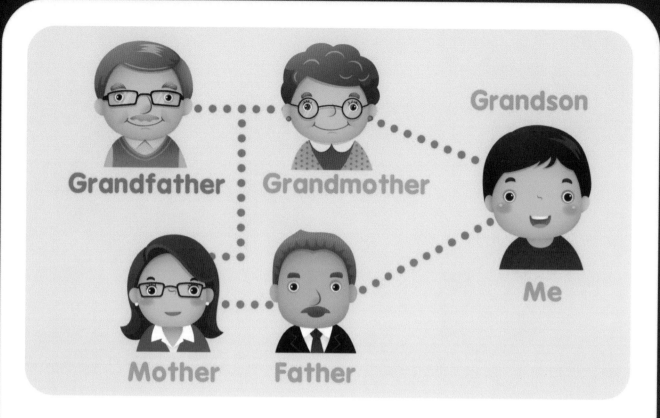

ปู่

Poo

Grandfather

ยาย

Yai

Grandmother

หลานชาย

Lhan - Chai

Grandson

สามี
Sa-Me
Husband

แม่
Mae
Mother

น้องสาว

Nong-Saw

Sister

ลูกชาย
Look - Chai
Son

ฝาแฝด
Fa - Faed
Twins

ภรรยา

Pan - Ra - Ya

Wife

Adjectives

สวย
Suay
Beautiful

น่าเกลียด
Nha - Klied
Ugly

ใหญ่
ynai

Big

เล็ก
Leg

Small

19

ว่าง

Vang

Empty

เต็ม

Them

Full

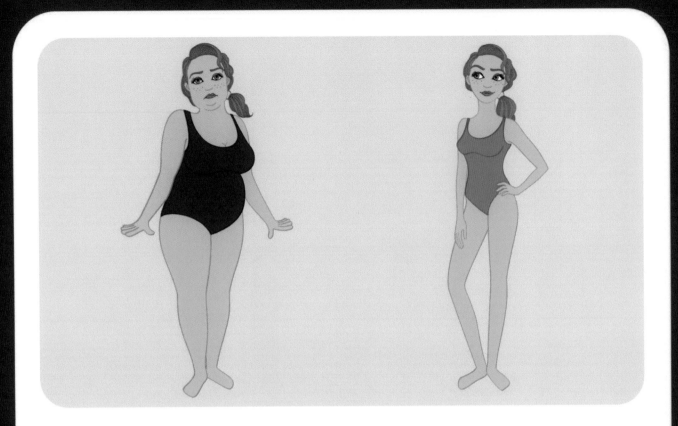

อ้วน
Uan

Fat

ผอม
Porm

Thin

มีความสุข
Mee - Quam - Sook

Happy

เศร้า
Souw

Sad

แข็ง

Kaeng

Hard

นุ่ม

Num

Soft

แนวนอน

Naew - Norn

Horizontal

แนวตั้ง

Naew - Tang

Vertical

ดัง

Dang

Loud

เงียบ

Ngieb

Quiet

แก่
Kae
Old

อ่อนวัย
Orn - Vai
Young

เปิด

Poed

ปิด

Pid

Open

Closed

เร็ว

Rew

Quick

ช้า

Sha

Slow

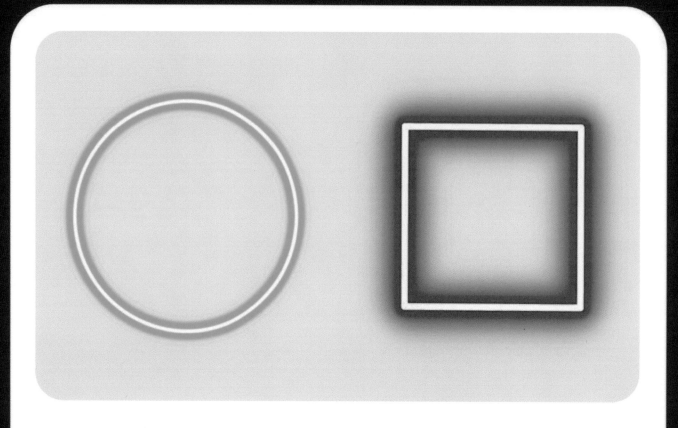

กลม
Glom

Round

สี่เหลี่ยม
See -Lhiem

Square

เตี้ย

Thie

Short

สูง

Soong

Tall

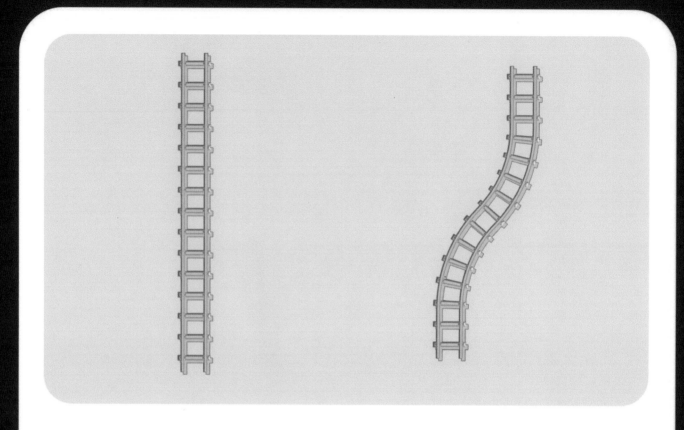

ตรง

Thlong

Straight

โค้ง

Khong

Curved

แข็งแรง

Khaeng-Raeng

Strong

อ่อนแอ

Orn - Ae

Weak

เปียก

Pieg

Wet

แห้ง

Haeng

Dry

กว้าง

Kuang

Wide

แคบ

Khaeb

Narrow

Printed in Great Britain
by Amazon

50999038R00022